MW01656953

Sexpectations

The Word says it all

Mike Novotny

Published by Straight Talk Books
P.O. Box 301, Milwaukee, WI 53201
800.661.3311 • timeofgrace.org

Printed in the United States of America
ISBN: 978-1-949488-25-8

Contents

Introduction.......... 5

Sex Is Good.......... 10

Sex Is Work.......... 26

Sex Is Fiery.......... 46

Sex Is Unnecessary.......... 66

Conclusion.......... 84

Introduction

Why would I want to write a book on sex? That's a good question. . . . I mean, not everyone who reads this is part of a perfect couple who's excited to practice what I preach! It's not a topic that's covered in church very much either. Why is that? Well, because there are little kids in church who seem too young to hear about sex. And there are teenagers in church sitting next to their parents; and if Dad would wink at Mom, those teenagers would die. And there are singles in church who might love to connect with someone sexually but can't just yet. And there are spouses in church who, like 15 percent of married people in America, have sexless marriages; this topic opens up old wounds. And there are many people who've been sinned against with sex. There are husbands and wives in church who've fought and argued and wept about sex, trying to figure out their differences in desires over the years. And there are widows and divorcees in church who miss the intimacy and connection of marriage, sex included. Isn't church about sin and salvation, not sex? Aren't we supposed to talk about the Bible and not about what goes on in the bedroom? Good questions. To which I have three good answers.

Aren't we supposed to talk about the Bible and not about what goes on in the bedroom?

I've talked about sex in church, and I want to write here about sex because THE WORLD IS. All the time. Listen to almost any song, watch almost any movie, and pick almost anything on Netflix; between pop culture and porn, we Americans are learning a lot about sex. What it is. How it works. Who should have it. And when. And how often. The Barna Research Group states, "With the ease of access to sexually explicit material today, and research showing the reluctance of parents to have candid conversations with their kids, young people are often left to their own devices (sometimes literally) when it comes to navigating the complex world of sex."[1] I studied the lyrics of the top ten songs on the radio and learned that real men and strong women are defined by how much loving they get from lots of people, not how much they choose to love one person. So, if all of us will get hundreds of messages about sex from the world, maybe we should get at least four chapters from the Word.

The second reason I want to talk about sex is because PARENTS AREN'T. I sent a survey about sex to my church members recently. Fifty-six people responded. The first question was, "Did your parents prepare you to appreciate God's gift of sex?" Six responders said yes. Eight said, "They only told me, 'Wait until marriage!'" And the rest said, "No. Never. We didn't talk about it." But that silence hurt us. Through the Time of Grace audience, I received tons of heartbreaking emails, especially from older women, about the damage done by the silence in our homes. One wrote, "I grew up in a strict Lutheran home. . . . Growing up, we never talked about sex. . . . I turned to other forms of educating myself. By the end of age 11, I delved into the world of pornography and attempted to teach myself. . . . The insistence that sex was shameful outside of marriage since I was a baby nailed me with so much anguish and guilt and self-hatred that I could not forgive myself for what I had done. So much so that I continued to live a life of promiscuity because I believed I was damaged. I believed there was nothing left of me. That I was ruined and could no longer be freed in God's eyes." In other words, not talking about sex in our homes and churches didn't bless us. It cursed us. With ignorance. With shame.

The final reason to discuss sex is because GOD DOES. What I'm going to share with you in this book are not articles from *Cosmopolitan* and *Maxim* but passages from Genesis and Song of Songs. From

God's Word. The Word we Christians believe is inspired by God. Every page. Every passage. Including the ones about sex. So if you want to read Bible teaching, I should probably teach about . . . sex!

Here's what I hope to share with you in these pages: Sex is good (not inherently dirty or bad). Sex is work (the result of real love, real connection, real effort). Sex is fiery (both powerful and dangerous at the same time). And Sex is optional (completely unnecessary for a satisfied life). I also want to remind you that sex is forgivable. This book is full of both grace and truth. Sound good? Then let's begin.

Sex Is Good

Some of you know about the night I thought I was being a good Samaritan . . . but actually I was picking up a prostitute. She was hunched over, shivering on a brutally cold Wisconsin winter night.

"Are you okay?" I asked out of my car window.

"No," she said, "my car just broke down at that gas station."

"Can I give you a lift home?"

"That would be amazing," she said as she hopped into my car.

I said, "Hi, I'm Mike," and we weren't a block down the road when she asked, "So, Mike, are you a freak?"

"Excuse me?"

"Are you a freak? Do you like to have sex?" (Remember that question as I finish this story.)

I said, "Yeah . . . with my wife."

She realized nothing was going to happen, so we talked about life and raising kids until she asked, "So, Mike, what do you do?"

"Well," I smiled, "I'm a pastor."

I wish you could have seen her face. "Just my luck," she groaned. I invited her to church on Christmas Eve, dropped her off, and had an incredible story for my wife the next morning.

Now go back to her question for a second: "Do you like to have sex?" That's a good question. Because it gets to the heart of what sex is. Can a Christian like it? desire it? enjoy it? Those are questions that go unanswered for most Christian kids. Because mostly what we hear in Christian churches and Christian homes is "Don't!" or "Wait!" Sex talks are awkward at best and often include shock-and-awe presentations of unwanted pregnancies and incurable STDs and the addictiveness of porn. In some families, you can't even say the word. Like a curse word, you can only spell it: S-E-X.

But the problems of this approach are immense. If all you've heard during your formative years is, "Don't! Sex is sinful! Shameful! Unchristian!" you've literally wired your brain to equate sex with sin. And getting married can't and won't flip that switch. If you've spent decades hearing (or assuming), "Good girls don't do that," then what will you think when you do that? So much of good sex is based on believing sex is good. The best sex is not a series of physical steps but the ability to be naked and unashamed. To be connected and comfortable. To be safe and loved. And none of that can happen unless we believe sex is, by its very nature, good.

You've literally wired your brain to equate sex with sin.

Which is why I want to take you back to the place where we first find sex in the Bible. In the beginning, before there was sin or shame, there was sex. And that sex was good. Look back at the first chapter of the Bible, Genesis 1: **"So God created**

mankind in his own image, in the image of God he created them; male and female he created them" (verse 27). God made man and woman, Adam and Eve, in his own image. That meant these people were like God; they were good like God, holy like God, sinless like God. In the beginning, God created two good people.

And guess what he did next? Right after the creation of human beings, the Word says, **"God blessed them and said to them, 'Be fruitful and increase in number'"** (verse 28). "Be fruitful. Increase in number. Have sex. You're welcome." We go from creation to procreation in one verse. And what does God think about his new creation? Three verses later, we read, **"God saw all that he had made, and it was very good"** (verse 31). What was very good? All that God made. And what did God make? Sex. Highlight this: SEX IS GOOD.

What was very good? All that God made. And what did God make? Sex.

This should be obvious, but we have this weird Christian culture that's scared of sex. We see the danger of sinful sex, so we only talk about the sinful side of sex. But there's another side. A good side. A godly side. And that side is where God starts. Just think it through: Who made our bodies? God! Who made the parts of our bodies? God! Who came up with the idea of sex? God! Who invented sexual pleasure? God! If you believe that God is good and if you believe God is the Maker of heaven and earth, then you believe, by your own confession, that sex is good.

A few years ago, a pastor preached a message called "Sex to the Glory of God," encouraging married couples to enjoy sex often as a way to praise and worship God. Sometime after the message, an older couple had the pastor over for dinner. They enjoyed a meal together, and then the wife gave the pastor the token tour of their home. She showed him the kitchen, the family room with the pictures of the grandkids, the basement, and the bedrooms. But she paused outside the master bedroom, smiled at the pastor, and said, "And this is the worship center." Yes! That Christian got it. Sex is not a necessary evil. Sex, when done selflessly between spouses, is worship. A way to tell God how much he is worth.

Nothing proves that point better than Song of Songs. Ever heard of it? It's tucked away in the Old Testament, but you should read it because it proves sex is not just for procreation but for recreation, for connection, for intimacy. Read 1:2: **"Let him kiss me with the kisses of his mouth."** That's quite an opening line. **"Take me away with you—let us hurry! Let the king bring me into his chambers"** (1:4). To play Fruit Ninja? Nope. For sex. To which their religious friends say in 1:5: **"We will praise your love more than wine."** No frowns. No shame. "Go for it!" their friends shout. And then you get to chapter 7: **"Your stature is like that of the palm, and your breasts like**

> *People are in so much pain in our society.*

clusters of fruit. I said, 'I will climb the palm tree; I will take hold of its fruit'" (verses 7,8). How's that for a life verse?! Parents, I know that's a bit much, but do you know what the father in Proverbs chapter 5 said to his son? **"May you rejoice in the wife of your youth. A loving doe, a graceful deer—may her breasts satisfy you always"** (verses 18,19). And God inspired him to say that!

What's the point? That sex is good. Yeah, we can mess it up. Yeah, we can make it selfish and scarring, but sex is not bad. Or wrong. Or dirty. Or demonic. Sex is from God. And God is good. All the time.

Sex is from God. And God is good. All the time.

So, what does this mean for us? Let's apply this teaching to three groups—singles, married couples, and parents. Singles, be carefully excited about sex. If you're dating or hope to be married one day, it's okay to be excited about sex. Coming up in chapter 3, I'll explain the "careful" part, because sex is fiery. For now, be excited. Look forward to it. You can be excited about one day marrying and having kids. And you can be excited about one day marrying and having sex. Because if God blesses you one day with marriage, he's going to show up at your reception, give his blessing to this gift, and smile, "You're welcome."

Married people, learn to see sex as good. If he wants sex or she desires sex, that's good. That's from God. Next chapter I'll talk about why good sex takes good work, why you can't make love without lots of nonsexual love first. For now start to talk about sex as something good. If talking about your bodies, your desires, or this part of your marriage feels awkward, that's okay. There are lots of good resources out there. Read and listen with discernment, but I'd recommend the book *Sheet Music*; the book *Friends, Partners, and Lovers*; and the podcast called *Sexy Marriage Radio*. Read, listen, and talk together about the good gift of good sex from a good God.

Parents, if you're married, tell your kids (with a smile) that Daddy and Mommy have sex. Let their first memories of sex not be porn or a playground story. Let it be, "Daddy loves Mommy. Mommy loves Daddy. Daddy and Mommy love sex." Of course, it will get awkward. When puberty hits and you try to talk about sex, your teenagers will want to stab themselves in the eardrum with a butter knife rather than listen—but they will listen. And they will remember. And when they see some cheap version of sex, some idiot who wants sex without love, they will remember what they've seen and heard at home their whole lives. Sex is something for people who have vowed to love and respect and say, "You first" until death do them part. That's what makes sex so good. Parents, scrap "the talk" and start to talk about sex. Your children, before you know it, will need it.

But no matter who you are, please know this: Sex is not just good; *sex is forgivable*. If you've made bad choices with God's good gift of sex, there's grace and forgiveness for you from Jesus. I know that because of a story Jesus told about a man who didn't just pick up a prostitute but had sex with her. And not just once. But when he came home to his father, alone and ashamed, when he confessed, "Father, I have sinned," Jesus said the father ran to his son and hugged him. He threw a feast and forgave him. The kid came home dirty and ended up dancing.

Do you know why Jesus told that story? So the sexual sinners in his "church" would know they were forgiven. And you are too. Confess your sins to Jesus, sexual sins included, and you can end up dancing. No guilt. No shame. No scarlet letter. Just grace. Just mercy. Just Jesus.

Study Guide

1. What did your parents and/or your church teach you about sex when you were growing up? Did they prepare you to recognize sex as a good gift from a loving God? If so, how? If not, why not?

2. Read Song of Songs and underline all the passages that prove that sex is a good gift from a great God.

3. On average, kids in America will be exposed to hard-core pornography by age 11. Before their first mouse click happens, what would you want to teach your children/nieces/nephews/etc. so that they see porn as a pathetic substitute to the amazing gift that God desires sex to be?

Prayer

Dear God, you are the Maker of heaven and earth. You knit me together in my mother's womb and gave me a body and mind with various parts. Please help me to believe in the goodness of the human body and in the divine design of sex. Rid my heart of anything sexually profane, hurtful, or shallow, in order that I might praise you for giving intimacy and connection as a gift to every married couple. I ask this in Jesus' name. Amen.

Journal

Father in heaven, when I remember that sex was your idea, it changes the way I think. It leads me to believe . . .

Sex Is Work

I wrote previously that there are three good reasons to talk about sex—because the world is, because parents aren't, and because God does. The world teaches us so much about sex, most of it foolish and fictional and dangerous. And most of our parents didn't teach us much about sex besides, "Don't!" or "Wait!" And God says so much about sex. On the first page of the Bible, God brings up sex. And things get steamy in the inspired book called Song of Songs. We've learned from God that sex is good. In the beginning, before there was anything bad, there was sex. A good God gave the gift of sex and said, "It is very good." That's our biblical foundation. Obviously, sex can go bad, but at its very heart, sex is not dirty or sinful or shameful. It's God's idea. Which means sex is good.

But some of you know sex isn't always good, even in marriage. When I sent that survey about sex to my church members, I asked, "If you could ask God any question about sex, what would you ask him?" The most common response was this: "Why are we so sexually different? Why does one spouse want sex more than the other?" Multiple people asked, "Why do guys want sex so much more?" It's not always the husband with the higher desire, but in almost every couple there is one who wants more sex than the other.

Which is a huge issue. There's something unique about sex that's so personal and powerful and emotional. When two people are on two different pages, sex can stop being good. The higher desire can feel rejected, disrespected, ignored, even unloved. If he or she is the only one who initiates sex, that person might wonder if he or she is desirable, attractive, or good enough. At the same time, the lower desire can feel pressured, exhausted, constantly trying but never satisfying. A couple with different desires can feel broken, messed up, incompatible.

Our culture doesn't help. The world of music and movies and Netflix shows us lots of sex, and that sex is easy. One flirtatious look, one raised eyebrow, one innuendo, and—boom—sex is happening. One author calls this "fiction sex," but the world doesn't warn us that way. Instead, it suggests good sex is natural, biological, eventual. So when sex turns out to be challenging or frustrating, you start to wonder what went wrong.

A couple with different desires can feel broken, messed up, incompatible.

I get that. Trust me. My wife said I could share this: The hardest part of our marriage has been this difference in desire. We have an amazing marriage—can I brag about it to God's glory? We try to pray every day, date every week, get away every quarter, and vacation every year. I make her breakfast every day. She packs my lunch before work.

We are on the same page with parenting, money, faith, and family. By God's grace, neither of us has endured sexual abuse and both of us were virgins until our wedding night. But guess where we were seven years into our marriage? A counselor's office. For what? To figure out how we could love each other so much but be so different when it came to sex. Over the years, we've learned so much and grown so much closer. But we would tell you that potty training and work/life balance have been easy compared to this. Here's what I really want you to know, even to expect: SEX IS WORK. Good sex, true connection and intimacy and pleasure, is work.

That's what the very first recorded sex in Scripture says. In the last chapter, we saw the invention of sex on page 1 of the Bible: "Be fruitful," God told Adam and Eve. "Multiply and make babies. Be naked but not ashamed." But we don't hear of sex actually happening until a few pages later. And the way God describes it is everything. Look at Genesis 4:1: **"Adam made love to his wife**

Eve." He made love. He didn't just have sex or (how would the kids say it?) get it on or get some or do the nasty or have relations or make whoopee or bow chicka wow wow (man, we have a lot of ways to talk about sex!). No, Adam made love. There is no good sex, God's kind of sex, without love. What is love in the Bible? Love is patient, love is kind, love is not self-seeking, love always protects, and love always perseveres. Love does what is best for the other, no matter what. Sex is bad when it's not good love. Which is why Adam made *love* to his wife.

But there's more. This passage was originally written in Hebrew, and the Hebrew literally says, "Adam yadah'd his wife." *Yadah* literally means, "He knew." It's the same verb as to know the answer to a question. Adam knew his wife, Eve. That's how the Jews would talk about sex. He knew her. The first time we see sex in the Bible is not just about pleasure or passion; it's about knowing someone.

This is why one author tells college students, "Your parents are better at sex than you are." That gets their attention! "My parents? Ew, and no way." Why would the students say that? Why would they think that they know more about sex than their parents? Because their world has taught them that sex is acrobatics, not intimacy; the shape of your bodies and not the state of your minds. No one has told them that the best sex is when a man "yadahs" his wife. Something that takes time, honesty, listening, forgiveness, and love.

Think of it like this. I've never played a violin before. Ever. I've never even held one. I've seen people play violins. I've even Googled "tips for playing violin." So, do you think if I picked up a violin and started playing that it would sound good? Of course not! We would never expect that. So why do we expect it from sex? Why would we use the phrase *honeymoon sex* as slang for the best sex ever? Why would we think hormones and passion and danger would make sex better than knowledge

He knew her. That's what made sex good.

and practice and love? No, God says Adam knew her. He knew her. That's what made sex good.

If you're married, I won't be giving many tips on good sex in this book, but I will say this: With sex, knowledge is power. Powerful sex happens when you know your spouse. When you've studied her for years. When you've learned what makes him tick. When is she most energetic and interested? In the morning? At night? After working out? When is she the least distracted? After her to-do list is done? After the kids are in bed? How spontaneous is he? Do you need to just go for it or give her time to prepare? Does talking or praying or cuddling make her more intimate? Does a flirty text during his workday spice things up? Is she a slow cooker or a microwave? Is his love language a compliment posted on Facebook or a back rub after work? Does doing her chores before she gets home (aka, "chore play") make her more interested in sex? Does she need tons of affirmation of her beauty after kids changed her body? Is he battling depression because of work stress and needing a morning distraction? This is what it means to "yadah." "I know you. Through the years, I know who you are and how you think and the best way to serve you, to love you. Which is why I know how to make love to you."

By the way, if you're dating, God wants you to start thinking about sex. This isn't just a time of "don't!" and "wait!" This is a time to learn, to study, to gain knowledge about yourself and maybe your future spouse. Talking and loving and serving one another in nonsexual ways gets you ready to, one day, have really good sex.

This makes me think of that turkey. A few years ago, I was on a field trip in Green Bay and saw these female turkeys pecking seeds for lunch. And who shows up during the meal? Tom Turkey. I should have taken a picture, because old Tom came in strutting—chest all swollen and feathers out. He strutted past all the ladies, did a 180-degree turn, and strutted past them again. And guess what? They didn't even look. Not a single lady turkey stopped eating! No lovin' for Tom that day. He didn't "know" those ladies very well.

Men, don't be that turkey. We dudes think taking off our shirts and flexing will do the trick, but that's because we're not "yadahing." We're forgetting that for most women, sex is mental. They have things on their minds, projects to finish, problems to think through. So, serve her well, and she can relax and let go, which is what makes sex good. Ladies, this is true for you too. Most men are visual. You can work like mad to have a beautiful home and a great family, but most men are visual. The way to our hearts is not through our stomachs. It's through our eyes. Remember that, and you can "yadah" your husband.

My favorite analogy about sex comes from a pastor who suggested a couple's sex life is like their child. Like a child, sex will take work and communication, mistakes and forgiveness. Like a child, sex will be incredible, have frustrating moments, and often be totally mediocre. And, like a child, a couple's sex is unique to them. No comparing yourselves to your friends' marriage or the average American couple. No, this sex is yours. Neglect your child or your sex life and it will come back to hurt you. Work hard together and this "child" will grow into something strong and

If you work together, it can be really good.

beautiful, something that bonds you and brings joy for decades to come. Expect sex to be work. But, if you work together, it can be really good.

Now I'm not just squeezing this idea out of one little word in Genesis chapter 4; Paul makes a similar connection in Ephesians chapter 5. On the other end of your Bible, Paul (who was joyful and satisfied despite not having sex, by the way—spoiler for chapter 4 to all you singles out there) connects sex with serving one another. Paul quotes Genesis 2: **"For this reason a man will leave his father and mother and be united to his wife, and the two will become one flesh"** (Ephesians 5:31). "One flesh" is a reference to the sexual and emotional union of husband and wife. But back up a few verses and Paul writes this: **"In this same way, husbands ought to love their wives as their own bodies"** (verse 28). Now men, how much do you love your bodies? Answer: A lot. You know your body, and you serve your body well. You know when your body is hungry or thirsty or cold or hot. And so you go to the kitchen, pour a glass of water, grab a sweatshirt, or roll down the windows. You "love" your body by meeting its wants and needs as soon as possible, which is how a husband is to love his wife. He comes to know what she wants, what she needs, and then tries to meet those needs and fulfill those wants as soon as possible. So, before Paul gets to one-flesh sex, he talks about love.

Which is how wives love their husbands. Ephesians 5:21: **"Submit to one another out of reverence for Christ."** *Submit* means to put someone else first. Put him first. Learn what makes him feel loved and how he likes to make love, and put him first. That's the good work that leads to good sex.

Which I think is the answer to your question: "Why are sex drives so different? Why does he want it more? Why aren't we exactly the same?" Here's my answer: So you can (make) love. Just like different personalities, different communication styles, different strengths force us to choose to love, sex is often the same way. Your spouse might be more or less interested than you are. Which makes sex your chance to love, to show how much she means to you, to serve him well. There are few things that matter more to God than loving your neighbor as yourself, even if your neighbor is the one you married.

But I can't say "Amen" until we talk about the most important teaching of all: *Sex is forgivable*. Because of Jesus, a virgin born of a virgin, sex is forgivable. Thank God. Because lots of us didn't do the work. And sex was not good. Not to God. We didn't do the work of waiting for marriage, waiting for God's timing. We didn't do the work of loving and serving, and we rushed it and pressured her. We didn't do the work of prioritizing and initiating, and he felt dismissed. So many of us have sinned sexually. But sex is forgivable. Paul told me so. Paul can't help but tell his Christian friends (who had major sexual baggage!) about Jesus. **"Husbands, love your wives, just as Christ loved the church and gave himself up for her to make her holy, cleansing her by the washing with water through the word, and to present her to himself as a radiant church, without stain or wrinkle or any other blemish, but holy and blameless"** (Ephesians 5:25-27). The "church" is you, every one of you who believes in Jesus as your Savior. Jesus gave himself up for you. Jesus made you holy. Jesus cleansed you in baptism and washed away every sexual sin. Jesus presented you radiant, not broken and not unworthy. Jesus sees you without stain or wrinkle or blemish. Jesus declares you holy and blameless.

Sex is forgivable.

Which means when you see him, he won't blame you. He won't shame you.

Because he already forgave you. Because Jesus did the work on the cross, the work of waiting and sacrificing and serving. He knew what we needed: someone to deal with our sins. He knew it, and he loved us enough to give it. So, yes, sex is good. And, yes, good sex takes work. But know this: No matter how good or bad sex has been for you, sex is forgivable.

Study Guide

1. Think of the last depiction of sex you saw in a movie or television show. What did it teach you to expect about the ease/difficulty of good sex? Did the people involved "know" each other, love each other, and respect each other? If not, why didn't the producers script sex more accurately?

2. Agree/Disagree: Selflessness is the key ingredient to good sex.

3. Study 1 Corinthians 13:4-8 and apply each description of love to the bedroom. How does this type of love elevate sexual intimacy to the beautiful height of God's original intentions?

4. Read Ephesians 5:25-27. What word from those verses would bring the most comfort to someone who feels ashamed for messing up God's plan for sex?

Prayer

Jesus, I praise you for doing all the work to make my relationship with God perfect. You selflessly served in order that I might experience the pleasure of God's presence forever, a feeling that will make even the best sex seem second rate. Today I ask for your Holy Spirit to produce in me the fruits of love, patience, gentleness, and kindness as I seek to honor you with my body. I know you will answer my prayer because I am praying today in Jesus' name. Amen.

Journal

Dear Father, if sex was easy, it would not grow me spiritually. The struggles I face in the bedroom are an opportunity for me to grow in . . .

Sex Is Fiery

Now I want to write about why, when it comes to sex, Christians are so different. I don't have to tell you that, right? Nowhere is the gap between Christians and our culture more obvious than the bedroom. The two agree on a few things, like consent, age, and maybe adultery. But on almost everything else, we have different answers. Can you hook up for no-strings-attached sex? Can you explore your sexuality through pornography? Can dating couples have sex? Or engaged couples? Culture says, "You can! You should!" But Christianity dares to say, "Not yet. Not until your vows. Sexual pleasure is a good gift that God only gives to a man and his wife." Which sounds crazy, right? Poor Christians are missing out on all the fun. No wonder people assume we're against sex.

By the way, this isn't new. Two thousand years ago, Christians were called out for being sexually different. Demosthenes, a writer from the 4th century B.C., described what that culture was like: "We have [concubines] for pleasure, female slaves for our daily care [sex] and wives to give us legitimate children." But not Christians. One man. One woman. One flesh. That's it. One critic of Christianity noted the difference: "[The Christians] share their food but not their wives." So, followers of Jesus have always been different when it comes to sex.

The same thing that warms and comforts also catches and destroys.

But just because it's clear in Jesus' teaching doesn't mean it's easy for Jesus' people. For some of my church family, this has been the hardest part about following Jesus. There are desires and urges that feel like needs. Saying no to lust, porn, premarital sex, and adultery can be agonizing. Trying to tell your date what you believe about sex can be a fast way to end a relationship. Working to not end up in the same place with your girlfriend is a struggle, a battle, a war. So, why would God do that? If sex is God's good idea and a way to find pleasure and connection, why would God limit sex for so few people to enjoy? Why would God ask us to live up to standards so few of us could keep? Why would Jesus ask you to be so different?

Good questions. And I found a good answer because I read every single Bible passage that uses the words *sex* or *sexual*. There are 77 total, almost evenly split between the Old and New Testaments, to believers living in B.C. Canaanite culture and A.D. Greek/Roman cultures. Guess what I found? Not 1 or 2 or 7 but all 77 passages are . . . warnings! There are lots of positive ways the Bible talks about sex, but when the word *sex* is used, 100 percent of the time God is warning us about the dangers of sex outside of marriage. Here's the point I want to explore: SEX IS FIERY.

In other words, God thinks about sex

like the fireplace in my house. We love making fires in our family room. The look of the flames. The warmth of the fire. A good fire on a cold night is the best. But that same fire scares me. When the fireplace door is swung open, I get nervous. Are my kids far enough away from the hot glass? Is there anything around that could catch on fire? And I'm not crazy to think that. Because fire is wild. The same thing that warms and comforts also catches and destroys. So I fear the fire. I know people who've gotten burned, who lost everything in a house fire. So I'm careful with it. As a father, I have rules about who can make a fire in our house and when and how. Not because fire is bad, but because fire is fiery.

Just like sex. Is sex bad? No. Should Christians never have sex because it might turn out bad? No. But should Christians have a healthy fear of sex wherever, whenever, with whomever? Absolutely. A loving Father wouldn't design it any other way. That's what I want to share with you here

3 of the 77 reasons why our Father warns us about sex. Like the passages, this will be pretty heavy, but my prayer is that, despite the challenge of obeying it and our regular need of forgiveness for it, you will trust God's countercultural design for sex.

The first passage comes from the book of Proverbs, which is an Old Testament book of wisdom. Proverbs portrays how wise people live. And Proverbs talks a lot about sex. In fact, for nearly three entire chapters a dad talks to his kids about sex. He affirms that sex is good (actually telling his son to enjoy his wife's body and be intoxicated by their love). But mostly this dad warns about sex gone bad. Listen to what he says about adultery: **"Can a man scoop fire into his lap without his clothes being burned? Can a man walk on hot coals without his feet being scorched? So is he who sleeps with another man's wife; no one who touches her will go unpunished"** (Proverbs 6:27-29). Notice the logic here. "I love you, son. I don't want to see you get burned. But sexual sin will burn you. No one who does it will go unpunished. You wouldn't dump a Weber grill's worth of burning coals on your pants. So, don't do this."

Why does this dad say this to his son? Why does he repeat it in Proverbs chapters 5 and 6 and 7? Why did God inspire so much ink on this one topic? A previous pastor at my church had this saying that stuck around, even years after he left. It said, "STP = LTP." Know what that means? Short-Term Pleasure = Long-Term Pain. Yeah, it will feel good now. It's sex! But the pleasure won't last. The consequences, however, will. This dad mentions shame, disgrace, and the fury of those who are hurt by our sexual sin. Why is God so restrictive? Because sex can hurt you.

Ever experienced that? Maybe you messed around with someone's boyfriend in high school, and it amplified the drama in *your* life. Maybe you were just having fun, and *you* ended up with an STD. Maybe you didn't plan to get pregnant, but *you* did. Maybe you believed your porn was private, but then *you* got caught or *you* got hooked or *you* didn't really know how real sex worked. Maybe you gave your body to a body who wasn't willing to work, to serve, to respect you, to protect you, and he broke *your* heart. Maybe *you* really messed up your family. Maybe *you* felt the shame of saying yes when you should have said no. Maybe you got naked and, though it was pleasure in the moment, it left *you* with pain.

God wants us to learn sexual self-control.

Many years ago, I taught a class of teens about sex. And, of course, one of the students brought a friend, his first time ever at our church (I'll call the friend Keandre). I didn't know Keandre's story or his background, but I sensed he didn't know much about the Bible. So the whole time I taught I was wondering what he thought about the Bible and sex. (I remember reading Song of Songs and seeing the expression on his face!) But when I paused and asked for questions, Keandre's hand went up.

"Yes?" I dared to ask.

"Pastor," Keandre shared, "the world would be better if everyone followed that. There would be no families who don't have a dad around."

Wow . . . this kid didn't know a lot about Christianity, but he knew our culture's habits hurt us.

Which is what God sees. Sure, some unmarried people could have sex and have fun. These proverbs aren't promises of stuff that happens every time. They are probabilities. I'm positive there are times when two people have sex and don't get hurt. Just like there are times when you leave the fireplace door open and the flames don't spread. Just like there are times you don't wear your seatbelt and are just fine. Just like there are times you don't look both ways yet cross the street in one piece. But God's mercy doesn't negate his wisdom. Because when we all think we'll be fine, when we all feel like we'll be the exception to God's rules, when we're convinced we'll just have fun and no one will get hurt, we do get hurt. Lots of us do.

But not just us. Sex can hurt others too. Check out God's second reason for being sexually cautious: **"It is God's will that you should be sanctified: that you should avoid sexual immorality; that each of you should learn to control your own body in a way that is holy and honorable, not in passionate lust like the pagans, who do not know God; and that in this matter no one should wrong or take advantage of a brother or sister"** (1 Thessalonians 4:3-6). God wants us to be sanctified, which means set apart from our culture, distinct and different like Jesus. God wants us to learn sexual self-control (and he said *learn* because that's not natural for most of us). God doesn't want us to see sex like pagans. Why not? Because "in this matter" (sex), you can wrong a brother or a sister. In other words, sexual sin doesn't just hurt you. Sex can hurt them.

That's what they told me. The biggest fear I had about talking about sex at church were the kinds of people who would hear it. Maybe a 20-year-old guy in church would be really interested in talking sex, but what about the 70-year-old woman watching on TV? But my fear went away after I asked people to email Time of Grace with any questions they might have about sex. Want to guess who emailed the most? Older women. Email after email of heartbreaking stories of sex that hurt. And I should have known that. Because that 70-year-old woman was 20 when the sexual revolution was hot and heavy, when America decided to keep the fire but dismantle the fireplace. And people got burned.

Maybe you know that too. Is there anything that comes close to the hurt caused by sexual sin? The affair, the addiction, the abuse? According to the National Sexual Violence Research Center, 1 in 3 women and 1 in 6 men will be victims of sexual violence.[2] And that's just sexual violence. Add pornography to the mix. Sit with me in my office as she cries, "I thought he was attracted to me." See the looks in their eyes as they try to recover from another relapse discovered in the search history. Porn kills. Because sex can hurt. Your short-term pleasure can cause them long-term pain.

But the biggest victim of sex isn't them or you. It's God. Look at our third reason: **"Therefore God gave them over in the sinful desires of their hearts to sexual impurity for the degrading of their bodies with one another. They exchanged the truth about God for a lie, and worshiped and served created things rather than the Creator"** (Romans 1:24,25). For the sake of sex, some of us give up God. We worship a created thing—sex—instead of the Creator—God. We trust in sex to make us happy instead of God. And that's how sex becomes our god. Sex can hurt him.

Christianity is different than our culture.

The worst thing that can happen in the bedroom is that you close your Bible. You stop listening to God. You exchange his truth for your truth, his wants for your wants, his Word for your word. And if someone tries to talk to you about the affair, the sex before marriage, the dating history, or your sexual identity, you won't hear it. Not even if Jesus said it. That's the proof. It's the proof you don't like sex or even love sex; you worship it. When you refuse to let the Lord get the last word, you are a sex slave. And, unless you change, you cannot be saved.

So, why would we change? Why would we let Jesus have the last word on sex? Why would we trust our heavenly Father if this Christian way is crazy? If the three reasons I've given don't convince you, here's something better: *Sex is forgivable*. When Jesus, who is God, came to this earth, he didn't hurt you. Despite all of your sins and your doubts and your sexual failures, he didn't hurt you. Instead he loved you, forgave you, and died for you.

That's what I want to tell this 20-year-old. She emailed me with her story: *"My boyfriend and I are both continuously going to church together, setting boundaries, seeking help, reading the Word together, and praying together; yet we keep engaging in sex, which leaves us both frustrated and convicted. . . . I feel dirty, guilty, and just unworthy of what God has for me. . . . I just don't know how God sees us right now, and I just feel so ashamed and like God is upset with us. Does he forgive people who keep engaging in the same sin although they claim to love him and follow him?"* Does God forgive people like that, people like us?

Despite the dark, rebellious part of our pasts, Jesus loves us. His cross put our sin to death, and his resurrection from the dead reconnected us to God. What Jesus did for us was so powerful and so perfect that this is how God feels about us. He is not ashamed. Not embarrassed. Not fed up. He knows your story, yet his love is unstoppable and unconditional. Christ gave himself for the church to make her holy, to make us so flawless God himself could delight in us.

Know this: Christianity is different than our culture. Not just with sex, but with salvation. Jesus may be cautious with sex, but he is crazy generous with forgiveness.

And grace. And mercy. And patience. And love. God knows this is hard, but our Father knows what's best for us. And the proof is in his Son, the Savior, who went through short-term pain so we can have eternal pleasure. Yeah, it might be hard to deny ourselves, to keep fighting, keep repenting, but where else would we want to be except with Jesus?

Study Guide

1. Think of the most sexually promiscuous person you know. Have frequent sex and multiple partners brought that person long-term pleasure and peace? Why or why not?

2. Study 1 Corinthians 6:12-20. List at least three reasons why Paul is so cautious about sexual immorality.

3. Evaluate: The Bible sets people up for guilt and shame by having such a high standard for sexual purity.

4. Spend some quantity time meditating on Proverbs 5-7, three chapters written by a caring father to his beloved son. Imagine that the father is your Father and that the son is you, God's child. How do these chapters reveal God's heart for you when it comes to his strict boundaries on sexual pleasure?

Prayer

Dear Father, it can be so easy to focus on short-term pleasure and forget about long-term pain, which is why I am so amazed by your Son, Jesus. He resisted every temptation to indulge in the moment. He resisted every sin that would have felt good in the present. He did all of that for me, so that eternal pleasure would be my hope, my for-sure future. Thank you for sending your obedient Son so that I never have to fear the fires of hell but, rather, can long for the joys of heaven. In Jesus' name. Amen.

Journal

Lord, thinking about tough topics today leads to wiser living tomorrow. Please guide me in the days to come as I . . .

Sex Is Unnecessary

Back in 2005, actor Steve Carrell of the *Office* fame played the role of Andy Stitzer, an electronic salesman, toy collector, and—as the title of the movie declared—40-year-old virgin. I don't remember much about the movie (I'm guessing it had its raunchy moments, so beware), but I do remember the picture on the posters: Carrell with his hair parted, a polo shirt, and a cheesy expression that was the opposite of cool. Which was the point. Because how could you be 40 and a virgin and cool at the same time? According to his friends, Andy's virginity was a problem to be cured.

There is much, much more to a satisfied life than sex.

Which is what our culture has told you. If you get through your third date or your first real relationship or high school or college or your 20s or—God forbid!—your 30s without sex, something must be seriously wrong with you. You're probably sexually repressed and frustrated and miserable. To our culture, happy virgins are like unicorns, fascinating creatures that can't actually exist. Bruno Mars says it best in his song "Locked Out of Heaven." He says sex takes him to paradise. He realizes that up until now and this sex, he's been locked out of heaven. Without sex, we're locked out of heaven. Locked out of a better place. Condemned to a sexless hell.

Now, my congregation doesn't sing Bruno Mars songs at church, but there's a hint of his beliefs among us. And that's likely true for you too. When we expect romance and marriage and sex to be necessary for a satisfied life. When we think people need pornography or masturbation or they'd die. When Jesus' words to *enjoy* (and not endure!) a single, sexless life seem crazy. Absurd. When having a prom date or Valentine's Day plans go from a nice thing to a needed thing. When we *have* to play matchmaker for our single friends, because not having someone must be . . . terrible. When our bachelor brothers and single sisters aren't admired for their unique part in the mission of God's church but instead pitied ("You'll find someone someday . . ."), something has gone wrong with the church. Very wrong.

Logically, it's wrong because happiness is so little about sex. Do the math. If you have sex every day for one hour (which would be a lot!), you'd spend only 4 percent of your week having sex. Does that make you 4 percent happy and 96 percent a repressed loser? Drop the sexy time to a more reasonable two total hours/week, and you'd spend about 1 percent of your week having sex and 99 percent on other stuff. So, almost all of us are somewhere between 0 to 1 percent sexually active and 99 to 100 percent sexually inactive. And yet we know we are not 99 to 100 percent frustrated and angry. Logically, we know there is much, much more to a satisfied life than sex.

But it's not just logical; it's biblical. I

want to introduce you to two guys from the Bible who prove this point: SEX IS UNNECESSARY. Unnecessary for happiness. Unnecessary for fulfillment. Unnecessary for satisfaction. I want to share the stories of two single men whose lives we want to be like despite the fact that they had zero sex.

The first man is named Paul, the dude who wrote about half of the New Testament. Look what Paul wrote about sex and singleness in 1 Corinthians chapter 7: **"Now for the matters you wrote about: 'It is good for a man not to have sexual relations with a woman.' But since sexual immorality is occurring, each man should have sexual relations with his own wife, and each woman with her own husband. . . . I say this as a concession, not as a command. I wish that all of you were as I am. But each of you has your own gift from God; one has this gift, another has that"** (verses 1,2,6,7). That's stunning! Bachelor Paul isn't throwing himself a pity party. He doesn't see himself as a pathetic 50-year-old virgin who wonders if the Corinthians have any single sisters.

Paul doesn't curl up with a pint of Ben & Jerry's and wish he had a wife like Peter. No, Paul dares to say, "I wish you all were like me. I wish you could live without sex. But not everyone has the gift." Catch that word? The *gift* of a good life without sex.

You don't need sex. What you need is God.

How could Paul be that happy about his relationship status? Paul knows and writes about the goodness of sex, so how could he be so cool without it? His words to the Philippians have the answer. **"Rejoice in the Lord always. I will say it again: Rejoice! . . . The Lord is near. . . . I have learned the secret of being content in any and every situation. . . . I can do all this through him who gives me strength"** (4:4,5,12,13). Paul was joyful always and content in any and every situation. How? Because he believed God was near. God was with him. The big, glorious, thrilling, interesting, amazing God was with him. Simply put, to Paul, God was better than sex. And he had God with him 100 percent of the time.

Author Trevin Wax explains it this way: "One of the reasons our society is so sex-saturated is because we are so transcendence-starved [that means we think so little of God]. Unable to reach the heavens, we go under the bed sheets."[3] Paul wasn't sex-saturated because he was transcendence-filled. He had God. Not a dinky, uninteresting-next-to-sex kind of God. But GOD. His identity was not in his sexuality but his spiritual status, a son who had 24/7 access to his Father in heaven. So Paul wasn't locked out of heaven. He had one foot in it. By faith he was already there. He lived life in the presence of God. He knew the face of his Father was shining on him and being gracious to him. He pictured the face of God, the God who gave him the constant joy that occasional sex could not.

Think of it like a piece of bread. You might be so hungry that you look at that bread and say, "I need that. I'm dying of hunger. I can't live without it." But that isn't exactly true. You need something—calories, energy—but it doesn't have to be the bread. The same with sex. We might think, "I need that right now," but we don't. What we need is connection, intimacy, pleasure, happiness, a place to go with our stress. Which is what God is offering in nonsexual ways. To connect. To know you and accept you. To help you deal with life. To make you happy. You don't need sex. What you need is God.

One day in the presence of God is better than one thousand days in someone's bed.

An old friend of mine once confessed that he liked going to strip clubs. I expected his reasons to be like most—the thrill, the danger, the pleasure. But that wasn't his reason. He told me he liked them because of the "temporary company." He wasn't searching for sex but for company, for connection, for attention. I have a feeling the girls who only said hello for money didn't fill the God-shaped hole in his heart. Because only God can. That is the secret. The secret of Paul, a sexless, satisfied man.

But Paul wasn't the first. The second proof that sex is unnecessary is the 33-year-old virgin we worship—Jesus. Garrett Kell once blogged, "Jesus . . . never had sex. Yet Jesus was the most fully human and complete person who has ever lived."[4] It's true. Fully man. And fully complete. Which is confusing to people who idolize sex. So confusing that centuries later people made up stories about a secret fling between Jesus and his friend Mary. "They had to have had something on the side. . . . I mean, Jesus couldn't have been that happy without sex."

But he was. Look at what Jesus prayed to the Father the night before he died, two decades after his body changed from boy to man: **"I am coming to you now, but I say these things while I am still in the world, so that they may have the full measure of my joy within them"** (John 17:13). "The full measure of my joy. My joy, my spiritual happiness, is not running on empty. It's filled up to the top, Father." Virgin Jesus didn't pray that he could be like us but that we could be like him. Joyful because of God's presence. Good with simply being with God.

And that's good news for all of us. You and I can use the unique blessings of our lives to remember how good God is (I call this idea a "This!" moment). When you say, "This! This is like being with God." And the more we think about "This!" the more we have the full measure of Jesus' joy.

As a husband and father, my wife and children give me lots of my "This!" moments. The joy I experience through date night, board games, pillow fights, and sex helps me realize God is glorious. But "This!" costs me a lot of time. About 30 hours of personal time a week (I counted). Which is 30 hours that a single Christian could experience "This!" in other ways. Single Christians have more time to grow in the Word, to travel and see God's nature in the natural world, to invest in amazing friends and enjoy amazing foods. Our "This!" moments might be different, but they all trampoline our hearts up to God, to the presence of the only one who can ultimately satisfy our souls.

This is the key to not being locked out of

"heaven." It's how to deal with impatience or bitterness or jealousy. Whether you find that someone or not, you can have a better connection, a better pleasure, a better life by seeking God. Psalm 84 says, **"Better is one day in your courts than a thousand elsewhere"** (verse 10). One day in the presence of God is better than one thousand days in someone's bed. Sure, sex is good. But it's not God. So, pray like Jesus taught: "Father, hallowed be your name. Let your name, the thought of you, be so hallowed, so holy, so wonderful, so different that sex would seem small and temporary and weak in comparison. Be so exalted, God, that the thought of you is better than the thought of anything on earth! Until the day I can enjoy sex. Or even if I never do again."

If you're married, this is massively important for a healthy marriage. If you think sex right now is necessary, you will sin against your spouse. You will pressure her for sex and pout when she doesn't want it. You will be desperate, which is never attractive. You'll whine instead of doing what leads to good sex. You will skip the working and the waiting and turn to porn or to an affair, which will burn you and hurt him or her. But if you've already found joy without sex. If your soul is already satisfied in God, then sex becomes unnecessary. Good, wonderful, "This!" but unnecessary. You will have learned the secret to being content. And you can wait until he's ready. Until she feels connected. Until you've done the work to make sex good. Which is the sexiest secret of them all.

Sex is good. But sex is not God.

No, I can't guarantee you'll have good sex this year. I can't guarantee you'll have any sex ever again. But I can guarantee that you can get to God. Why? Because I know a 33-year-old virgin who unlocked the door to heaven. I know a Savior who offers everything you need to satisfy your soul. I know a Jesus who promised the kind of joy that would last long after the high of sex has worn off. Why? Because *sex is forgivable*.

Thank God for that. At my church, there

are so many times we want God to forgive and forget. So many things done to us. So many things we've done. I remember one Christian sharing his story and saying, "Pastor, I hope you see me as a human being and not as a terrible sinner." I told him, "I don't see you as either. I see you as a saint." Because that's what Jesus sees. He sees us as saints because we've been saved. Jesus makes us pure and holy and good enough to stand in the presence of God without guilt, without shame. Because hours after he prayed that prayer, "Father, fill them up with the full measure of my joy," Jesus went to a cross so that the prayer would be answered. So that we would be forgiven for every sin, sexual sins included. So that we could come to the Father through Jesus the Son. So we could boldly approach his throne, blameless now—yes, now!—and running home.

Jesus Christ lived a joyful life and died on a cross so that you could live with joy. You could live every day knowing that God is with you always. That you are loved always.

That you have a thrilling purpose always. That a day is coming when you will feel a kind of happiness no sexual encounter could provide. Sex is good. But sex is not God. You might not have sex. But, because of Jesus, you have everything you need.

Study Guide

1. Agree/Disagree: Americans are obsessed with sex because they've stopped being obsessed with God.

2. Read Philippians 4:4-13. How do Paul's words affect your answer to the Agree/Disagree statement above?

3. Study David's words in Psalm 16. How does God's presence make sex unnecessary for our eternal pleasure?

4. List your top three takeaways from this book. Share them with a trusted Christian friend as you encourage each other to celebrate sex as a good (but unnecessary) gift from God.

Prayer

Gracious Lord, you have taught, challenged, inspired, convicted, and comforted me in many ways through this book. Please give me wisdom to know what to do with what I've read. In these confusing times, let my life be an example of faith, purity, and the freedom that only Jesus can give. I ask this all in my Savior's name. Amen.

Journal

Father, sex so often feels like something I need to be happy. But today I cling to the promise that your presence is all I need to rejoice and have peace. I am particularly grateful today for your . . .

Conclusion

Talk about sex? Yes. We have to talk about it because our world is, our parents aren't, and our God does. How will Christians know what's right and good and true and meaningful if the only expectations we have come from people who don't know us like our family or love us like our God? How will we know that we belong here and in heaven unless someone tells us Jesus died to erase sexual sins, to forgive us too? So, remember that

- Sex is good. Not inherently bad or shameful or embarrassing or taboo. Sex is good, because sex is God's idea. The Creator's brilliant way for couples to connect.

- Sex is work. The best sex is the result

of two people working hard to know, love, respect, and serve one another.

- Sex is fiery. Christianity is different than culture because, like fire out of a fireplace, sex can burn you; it can hurt you, hurt them, and hurt your relationship with God.

- Sex is unnecessary. You can have a better connection, a better pleasure, a better life by seeking God.

- And thank God that sex is forgivable. Jesus hung out with sexual sinners. He ate with them, loved them, died on the cross and forgave them. We are all forgiven.

Notes

[1] "Should Sex Ed Teach Abstinence? Most Americans Say Yes," September 5, 2017, https://www.barna.com/research/sex-ed-teach-waiting-say-yes/).

[2] https://www.nsvrc.org/node/4737

[3] Trevin Wax, "Sex Is More AND Less Important Than You Think," August 11, 2015, https://www.thegospelcoalition.org/blogs/trevin-wax/taking-sex-more-and-less-seriously-than-the-culture/.

[4] Garrett Kell, "Good Lovemaking Is About God," July 11, 2017, https://www.desiringgod.org/articles/good-lovemaking-is-about-god.

About the Writer

Pastor Mike Novotny has served God's people in full-time ministry since 2007 in Madison and, most recently, at The CORE in Appleton, Wisconsin. He also serves as the lead speaker for Time of Grace, where he shares the good news about Jesus through television, print, and online platforms. Mike loves seeing people grasp the depth of God's amazing grace and unstoppable mercy. His wife continues to love him (despite plenty of reasons not to), and his two daughters open his eyes to the love of God for every Christian. When not talking about Jesus or dating his wife/girls, Mike loves playing soccer, running, and reading.

About Time of Grace

Time of Grace is for people who want more growth and less struggle in their spiritual walk. We share the truth of God's Word simply and clearly through television, print, and digital media that people view millions of times each month. We connect people to God's grace so they know they are loved and forgiven and can start experiencing a joy-filled life no matter what challenges life brings.

To discover more, please visit timeofgrace.org or call 800.661.3311.

Help share God's message of grace!

Every gift you give helps Time of Grace reach people around the world with the good news of Jesus. Your generosity and prayer support take the gospel of grace to others through our ministry outreach and help them find the restart with Jesus they need.

Give today at timeofgrace.org/give or by calling 800.661.3311.

Thank you!